MW00963894

Stone + Fist
Brick + Bone

john jeffire

AQUARIUS PRESS
DETROIT, MICHIGAN

Stone+Fist+Brick+Bone by John Jeffire

ISBN   978-0-9718214-0-8
LCCN   2008925223

The poet wishes to thank the editors of the following sources for publishing his poems: *Holla* ("Shooting Pool With My Daughter the Day After Her Release from Rehab)"; *thedetroiter.com* ("Personal" and "Small Man on the Skeleton Crew Down at Olympia Stadium"); *English Journal* ("Lionfish" and "In This Poem I Will Tell"); *The Peralta Press* ("Reading Between the Wire"); *Into the Teeth of the Wind* ("Panties", "Green Cologne", and "Routes"); *Poets' League of Greater Cleveland Chapbook* ("Those Days"); *America* ("Morning"); *Foxtail* ("The Age Demands"); *Millstream Valley Press* ("Welcome"); *South Coast Poetry Journal* ("Angel"); *Ex Libris* ("Wedding Day"); *Negative Capability* ("Lea Nicole").

Cover Art: Lea Jeffire

AQUARIUS PRESS
PO Box 23096
Detroit, MI 48223
(313) 515-8122
aquariuspress@sbcglobal.net
www.aquariuspressbookseller.net
www.aquariuspress.blogspot.com

Printed in the United States of America

This book is for Tracey,
Lea, and Jake:

What thou lovest well remains.

CONTENTS

Those Days

The chemical-orange River Rouge
sun was an overgrown uncle
slipping me a sip of Stroh's
and it took weeks to journey
the stone's throw home from school.
Ripping fistfuls of flowers
through chainlink for my mother
from anybody's garden
the East End alleys were
jeweled highways lined
with garbage can guards
where I once untombed
a baseball bat, a handgun,
and a stack of Hustlers.
I sang songs in German and Japanese,
Sukiaki and the girl from Ipanema,
kicked jams with a devil in a blue dress,
outdrew Boyd and Brown
and gunned them down,
entertained Captain Bob-Lo and Tricky Dick,
hat-tricked Gordie Howe,
kayoed Cassius Clay and Blue Lewis,
was crowned King of Dearborn
by Orville Hubbard.
When rain machine-gunned
our aluminum awning
and left me penned on the porch,
I took being wet, nameless, and small
because the factory haze sun
always returned with no hard feelings
lighting me to the treasure
of my world.

My Language
(Upon Being Told I Make No Sense)

So hire a translator, I say,
Always with my answers,
But don't look at me
Because not even I speak
My own language, English
Or Polish or Swedish or
Frenchish or any other –ish,
(well, maybe gibberish, but
So few of us speak it with
Such eloquence anymore).
Start with my deceased grandfather,
Who once tried to feel-up
My brother's first fiancé
In the darkened hallway
Of our apartment and,
When confronted, defiantly
Declared, "I wouldn't spend
A dime on that hussy."
Or maybe the sloshed Slavic blond
At the polkafest who was
Well into her boombas but
Not so much so to inform me
Upon my proposal to dance,
"Leetle mon, I'm note dat dronk."
Or perhaps Diamond John
The shift foreman at the butchershop
Who cleavered and filleted our souls
On a daily basis and fired me
For ineptitude not even I could deny
With the words, "Hate to skin ya,

Partner, but I need your hide."
Take their tongues and wring them dry,
Soaked vinegar rags twisted into cyclones
Of non sequitur, dripping the perfect sense
Of crashed syntax, godly nectar of nonsense,
My piss-poor gift to raise eyebrows like
A tuxedoed magician floating a hokey maiden,
And there, there, right there is my language.

6423 Coleman Avenue

No armored horde stormed our two-story walls,
but we did wage nightly war with
hockey sticks and a BB-gun against
whiptailed alleyrats the length of our arms.
Without a tennis court for oaths,
we stickballed bald tennis balls
in the backyard with a beheaded broomhandle
and plotted knuckleball revenge when we lost.
No holes were snipped in our chainlink fence
to receive a conquering champion,
but on the frontporch one morning we did find
a comatose drunk wandered from the
OK Corral Saloon, canadian clubbed in his quest
for a boilermaker grail.
Not one demented hag lurked the upper flat,
just the red-faced tenant from Arkansas
who threatened to skin the family dog for barking.
And the only impassioned cries for unity
delivered from the ramparts of that porch
in the colonial wilds of East Dearborn were,
"Dinnertime, Johnny Joseph, you get
your little ass home right this minute!"

Angel

He gallops a three year old skip,
soft bare feet slapping the sidewalk,
dimpled arms rhythmically moving the air,
chanting, "This is Heaven! I'm an angel!"
His father's ringed in grease at the plant,
won't be home till six, and Mama's
lulled by April air, coldcuts, and a beer—
so diaperless Kubla Khan, feeling the earth
pitty-pat beneath his feet, arms parting the air,
exclaims in the pure pinnacle of wisdom,
"This is Heaven! I'm an angel!"

The Age Demands

Walt Whitman split the wood,
you came to carve it,
and now we are left
      with the face of things—

    but the metaphor:

    shall we keep carving
          whittle the image

              an axhandle

   look away
       turn to stone

       demand all

   bonfire of commerce

My Best Friend's Old Man
—for Pete Greco

A snubnose filterless
crouches his purpled lip,
and when the smoke curls
back into his squinted eyes
you can't tell if he's
Dean Martin or Lon Chaney.
On the drive to the Carmen Theater
we listen to WJZZ,
Detroit's all night jazz,
his knuckled fingers
tatta-pattatta-patting
the steering wheel
to a mysterious, wordless song.
We sit quiet without being told.
He brakes the car
under running neon.
He looks all ways,
passes his son a five
like some secret pay-off,
then reaches, further,
touches his cheek.
We come alive, scrambling
from the cavernous backseat
into the cinema billboard,
Frankenstein and James Bond,
so different than
the aftershave and cigarettes
of the black car.
He waves us off
to the ticket booth,

scowling, grinning,
says he'll be back
at 9:15, on the nose,
you kids don't go nowhere, you hear?
Then the car gleams away,
as black and shiny and bulletproof
as the old man's hair,
ya-pattatta-pattatta-poom.

Closing Time

Last call a half hour gone,
my father ordering me
to lean on the mop handle
and my wanting to lean
until I felt it snap
easy as a cap twisted
from another customer's beer—
I labored in the family bar
beneath the autographed Gordie Howe,
'68 Tigers, Muhammed Ali,
and 3-foot high Elvis,
listening to change skip
from my mother's counting hand,
and the bar floor
came clean like it did
the night before,
but somewhere beyond
the last stoned stragglers
and tomorrow's deposit
the world rolled slowly about
the sun without us.
I remember trying to sleep
in our apartment above the bar
with mice and roaches
seeping through the walls
from the tenement next door,
Columbus and Wheeling bound semis
quaking the walls of my room
above the sleeping kegs and ashtrays,
laying on a sheetless mattress
with no bedstand

wishing I had someone to hate
for too many nights
the register rang out light,
the same bowl of cereal
each morning, and the cigarette soot
and bar floor stink I took to bed
no matter how many times I washed.
Drowning to sleep
as the sun broke the blinds,
the morning's last semis
mumbling in the bare brick walls,
I dreamed I would
one day hold enough money
to buy my freedom,
find a woman to lay with me
in a clean, soundless room,
look out a smudgeless window
at a road of my own leading to
a place I knew I should be.

The Ghost
—for my grandfather

We must forgive the dead,
Who can no longer hurt
Without our consent.
The only pain left
Is that which we embrace
Stoking the embers
As they try to burn off
Like morning fog.
Bitterness is this ghost
Who now sits at a table
We refuse to set—
Waiting, nowhere to go
Until we face him,
Until our living breath shreds
Him like a gale,
Until our eyes stare
Him into nothingness
And the dead are invited
To find their place.

Green Cologne

Only the green cologne for me,
the last bottle at the end of the shelf,
the important half-gallon size.
Effective as aspirin, I laugh,
potent as electrocution,
it's pitched in manly truth:
its pungency caught me a wife
quicker that cablevision,
and my son now emulates me,
scaling toiletseat and sink
to attain the green nectar,
annointing himself and the cats,
baptising toothbrush heads,
exploding our home
with piney, limey genius.

Think what you want.
I have more friends.
I am something
not even I can describe.
I bend oncoming automobiles
with a splash of green charm.

The Good Soldier

The answers of the captured
Double agent arrive too quickly,
Too easily, too well rehearsed.
The emergency room physician
Is not a skilled interrogator.
The swelling golfball bulging
From my forehead?
Kid never pays attention.
Walked right into a counter
At K-Mart, wham,
Never even saw it coming.
And the arm that dangles
From my left side,
Hanging like a stroke
Victim's useless limb?
Hell, I tried to help him up
The stairs but he never
Pays attention, so I tried
To help him up the stairs,
But he pulled away
Just when I pulled
To help him and, pop,
Out come the arm.

After release at Dairy Queen,
He tells me I am tough.
You never cried, man.
You took it like a soldier.
You kept your mouth shut.
That's a good man.

I am five years old but
I'm a good man.
You woulda never got it put
Back into place if we didn't
Notice how you couldn't lift it up.
You're lucky we care about you.
I am lucky. I am cared for.
My father says I'm tough.
I wear my sling proudly.
I will never leak a word
That betrays pain to the enemy.
Pain is our secret sign.
We keep it under wraps.
Name, rank, serial number.

I am a grown man now.
The cartilage in my chest
Never healed properly and
A mass of scartissue forms a
Permanent, disfigured wall
Over my purpled heart.
Here, run your hand over
The ripped terrain of my duty.
I am the veteran who doesn't
Answer the reunion invitation.
Sorry, but I have nothing to say
Except what is in this poem.
The mass of scabbed memory
Clumped off my left breastbone
Is no public badge of honor.

Panties

Courtship flowered ripe
fruit of the loin
blooms of cancun blue
satin silk petal
plunging swelled bikini belly
dripped hyacinth nectar
stiff wing brushing
heavyhung lilac

Marriage thrilled sugar lace
string hipped snowflake
frilly sweet secret
pristine Queen Anne threaded
on a bed of pearl

Parenthood, children asleep,
tiger, fire-engine, astronaut,
we peel away unseen,
a universe of fingertips,
elastic band catching
the knots of your ankles

Morning

I wake
before my wife
and daughter
and stare
at the ceiling,
then pull myself
up to sit
on the edge
of the bed.
Momentarily caught
in the dresser mirror,
the lean definition
of muscle and bone
is wearing away,
less imposing,
but smoother,
perhaps more graceful.
Seven hundred miles
away in Detroit,
my uncle's second wife
sips her final
shallow breaths
and I rise,
lightheaded, finding
the morning's equilibrium,
opening like a flower
in the constant
faceless breeze
that calls it
to the earth.

In This Poem I Will Tell You
About the Luncheon Following
The Final Day of Class at the
2004 Meadow Brook Writers Program

Bravo's, upscale Italian
bowtied waiters, salad forks
20 or so of us, teachers
writers, whatever

a few brewskies and I decide
I want to eat only appetizers
because, I don't know,
just because
I want to eat appetizers

and during my second appetizer
Shirley asks me,
"What's that, John?"

and I say, "Calimari,
highclass junkfood."

And Pamela looks at me still
so I say, "Little squids"
and I find a whole teeny squid
deep-fried into perfect petrification
and I hold him up by a tenticle

and the ladies smilefrown

and I think I could

chase Shirley and Pamela
screaming around the restaurant
with my squid

Introducing Myself to My Students
at the Allen Correctional Institute
on the First Day of Class

My name is John Jeffire and this is College Writing I.
You may call me Mr. Jeffire or you may call me John...
Or you may call me Big Bad John the Big Bossman,
John the Baptism under Jeffire, the man who knew modifiers,
Trustee of Truth, Deputy of Diction, Warden of Wordchoice,
The one man cool hand chain-gang grammar brain,
Little Johnny blowing on the comma-trombone—

And if a one of you raises a word to strike me,
I will call myself your teacher.

Hunger

When I was a small kid
We ate mayonnaise sandwiches
On tasteless Wonderbread
And washed it down with Kool-Aid
That never had enough sugar.
"Why can't we drink pop?"
My brother would protest,
Dreaming of carbony Coke and
7-Up as he grimaced down
The bitter, tinted water.
"That costs money," my mother
would always say, with neither
guilt, shame, nor pride in her voice.
She cut our sandwiches into
Four crusty triangles, "stars"
She called them, a ploy that I later
Realized was designed to make us
Believe we were eating four times
As much as we actually were
And when the last sweet, sour mash
Of sandwich slid down our throats,
All that was left to fill our bellies
Was the soft, chlorine scent
Of the flavorless white bread
Clinging to our fingertips.
Today, I eat out with my family,
And I order them to order
Whatever they want.
I am somewhat embarrassed that
I eat everything on the plate short of

Toothpicks and condiment cups,
Every sesame seed and carrot sliver,
Every pickle spear and hash brown flake,
Even the little leafy garnishes only
Meant for decoration, never
Paying the bill until I've filled
Myself and savored every last
Bitter, indivisible, paid for crumb.

Reading Between the Wire

Crushed sockets blackened eyes
Hope caverns like sunken cheek
Skinless fingers bone the wire—

Now, unwrite the rib chimneys
Today, lime the blind eye
Shovel fleshy dirt, innocent ash
Rake the bone roached
echo of a hollow boot

   —*Oswiecim, 1992*

In This Story
(on a theme by Levine)

No dumbfriendly neighbor grins
from the porchswing, weakly waving
as you skip home from school.
No grandma offers you coffee sweet
with sugar and cream in your favorite cup.
No big sister lets you steer
the fenderless Nova in the school lot.

In this story, he sits in a car
across the street and down the block.
He wears bottlebottom glasses
and smells like smoke and brown teeth.
He's been there all year—
he followed you to school.
He watched you, you saw him,
but you can't ever tell mom or dad
you took the ride home.

Even now.
You burn but can never get even.
Kill him, even if you could find him,
and it's you who does time.
Even now, you smell him pull
at your shiny belt
and your pants swivel around
your body like a noose.

Small Man on the Skeleton Crew
Down at Olympia Stadium

You looking at me?
What makes you think
I can't pop
your eyes out your head,
squeeze your windpipe,
drive a nail
through your eardrum?

You know it,
I'm nothing for
anyone to scare at—
I'm a small man,
couldn't do you
no harm, it's true—

but I'm bigger than your children
and I know where they play

Serotonin

Without you, life mumbles
Like stale stink that stumbles
From pawn shop to liquor store

In me, corners lurk corners, shadows
Broken street lights and unmade widows
Lead paint peeling from lidless windows

Aimless, reason leak, no valves, connectors
Winded, kill switch, fear the denominator
Uncommon, gunned lipless infiltrator

Hands leaf like earth tremor shock
Handleless door closed and locked
Rudderless thought adrift, tip, bob

No roads not taken, less traveled
Direction lost, flood gut unraveled
Lost in my own eye, shoeless foothold

Diamond fix, the trick to swallow you raw
Before I werewolf, little blue rabbit paw
Bar the doors to looney freak and claw
Sleep the loose goon tooth come dawn

Whiskey

We learned your lightning young
When mother rubbed you
Onto a teething gum.
Later, every bousha knew
To Seven Crown the winter flu,
Stewing the amber elixir
And common cold fixer
With honey, lemon, and tea,
The trusted cure-all hot toddy.
As adults, women sipped classy Manhattan
And ate pierogis at polkafests in Hamtramck
With rye and gingered men who'd forgotten
The sweat, sludge, and vodka of Gdansk.
Later, cause or effect, no one asked,
You balmed straight up a spouse gone cold
Or rang in Roman unions with rings of gold
And made grown men bold enough to dance
In the wee hours at a K of C bash.
Chased by a draft in habits that blurred,
We curl in your learned comfort, assured
That as long as we taste your life burned
Upon our tongues, we are here, returned
Another day, your scent on our drifting breath
80 proofs you are spirit of life, spirit of death.

Welcome

Mama warned him
at the inspection house:
keep the festering boil
on his ribs hidden
or be herded back
into the damp gut
of the ship alone.
But here, somewhere
in the new world,
too many nights
and how many days
from the island
of the star-headed lady,
the smell of dung and hay
and Mama's dress
the only remnants
of Polska—here,
as his five year old frame
is lifted from
the horse-drawn wagon
by the man who is no color
anyone has ever been before,
as he is suspended
in the blistering pop
of the burst boil,
the red rub of pain
too much, he cries.

The leather-skinned man
sets him to earth,
touches his head, speaks

sounds that are no words.
Mama hurries, smothers
the childish sobs,
the teared, snotty ache
of the burning side.
Across the street,
Papa watches from the crowd,
cracked, coaled hands crossed
in the stiff small of his back.
So, this is his son, the boy
he paid good money
to bring over, the one
who will help so much.
Hurry, quiet him down.
Let's make this welcome over.

Routes

Thumbing the family atlas
before a business trip,
I find four year old Lea's
travelled Nevada
with a pine green crayon.
Bold, indelible curlycues
now ring Reno and Carson City,
then loop southeast to Vegas,
where once, years ago,
a longsincelost cousin of mine,
seventeen and pregnant,
wed a blackjack dealer.
Just yesterday, my first child,
my only daughter, puzzled
above a baloney sandwich,
deciding whether to marry
Brandon, the neighbor boy,
or Jason, a playmate at daycare.
"Brandon," she then asserted,
"Most definitely Brandon."
I linger a moment in Nevada,
follow her green path as it twists,
wanders through the Proving Grounds,
scrambles north along I-93
toward the Idaho line,
so quick, so curvy, so unstoppably green
I'm still not exactly sure
what route she's taking.

Your Witness

I'm a 16-year-old white male
and I am in the backseat
of the family's rusted blue
Pontiac LeMans, Ohio plates.
I have never been on a date before
but I am now lying on top of Lisa,
who has cheeseburger-
peppermint-schnapps-vomit
tangled in her hair.
She appears to be breathing.
My penis is a crowbar
made of cotton candy.
I have no idea what I'm doing.

Next morning, Dad needs the car,
So he'll drive me to work.
One last meal: I'm led to the scene.
He cracks the driver's side door.
"Goddamn, what the fuck?"
he deduces insightfully,
introduced to exhibits A and B,
the smell of cheeseburger schnapps,
the makings of a murder.
"Ahhh?" I counter, my cross exam,
my index finger curling my chin,
gathering a look more
perplexed than algebra.
"What if your mother saw this"
he tells the court as the bailiff is called.
"Ummm," I offer in summation,
raising my hands in defense,

my final character witness noosed
without sentence on the stand
in a web of Roman Catholic guilt—
the plea is no contest and, God,
please, no further questions

Terminal
—for my father

Charred winter clouds browed above
stale burnt lung anger gust
damp soles, clothing crisped cold
bone froze, ache, muscle numb
each snowflake, lost second, moment
mounded time drifting
glare road, cracked icicle jaw
decayed breath frozen solid

      blown bit by bit
      snow by mind by time
      white eyed good-bye
      raw burn skin kingdom come
      here, nothing that is
      nothing that is not
            nothing....

Easter dinner
the family holding hands at grace
"Bless us, dear Lord, for these thy gifts..."
my father's hand warm
summer fish belly
not the hand that eight-balled downtown
dry, thick mop handle callouse
Johnny Walker Red and water and screw you
hair chemo patched, field hacked
by demented scythe
black sea weathering sixty two years dried away
his father, my son and daughter, our wives
ringed around a rosary, a ham, lit candles

this meal, we know, can only last so long
we know, can feed so many
"...through Christ, our Lord, amen"

      That moment
      scale skinned
      snow ashing the sky
      in two weeks you are gone
      leafless cracked wind
      shroud of misted breath rising
      thaw pacing
      our splintered house

Suburbanite

Man the porch.
Fist your chest
to the seigers
on the cul-de-sac.
Teeth snare the light
of moon and
sentry fires,
glint polished shields,
rearview mirrors,
satellite dishes.
The bastards.
All of them.
Blade their throats,
let the doorbells ring
as eyes clutch
an Ambien sleep—

When God looses
the morning sun,
time unhinged,
the mad chariot righted,
patent leather shoes
click the walk
and turbo engines
hum FM public radio news.
You smile the neighbors.
The drywalls have held again.

Wedding Day

When the bowtied band
that no one danced to
packed and slipped away
and the crumbs of the
crayon cake had dried
on the last paper plate,
we ditched the K of C hall.
Two hundred miles later,
Costello's Motor Inn held
Kingston's last vacancy.
I watched you undress
under the bare lightbulb
in the closet bathroom,
then shared warm Cold Duck,
ignoring the TV as it annoyed
the dying air conditioner.
When the champagne bottle stood
the sill with a carryout twelve,
the blue beams of Mr. Costello's
neon reputation said it
was time to draw the curtains
and take off my shoes.

One room over, laughter.
I look at you as you look at me.
We have been together
longer than we can know.

Walking the Dog

Last night's beer and barf
and half-eaten corned beefs
fester in the alley behind the family bar
while my 20 year old terrier limps
next door to Eddie's Quick Lube.
He noses in and out
of empty motor oil drums
and crating, finally finding
a gutted engine block,
which he squirts.
The dog looks up the alley
and sniffs what his
glazed eyes cannot see.
He senses me yelling
at him to come on
so I can get ready for my shift
behind the bar, but he disobeys.
On an island of weed and tall grass
next to the telephone pole
he hunches, bone tail straight,
ears back, he begins the firmest
dump he has taken in months.
My deaf animal, older than I am,
his once soft whiteness
bristly and yellowed, his blackness
specked with white, is saved
from crapping in the apartment,
my father's rolled paper and a pointing finger.
He looks up at me with
cataracted eyes and I touch his head
and tell him

"Good Boy" as we head back
to the fire escape.

Tenements heavy with the ache
of package store bladders
empty themselves.
I get a whiff of something
beyond our dumpster.
Ragchildren hang from the balconies,
waiting for me to leave
so they can scavenge our garbage
for tin, aluminum cans, bottles
and crushed cardboard castles.
I turn to herd the blind dog
back up the fire escape,
and one mudheaded girl
peaks from behind the dumpster,
picks at sandwiches on the ground.
A snake of smoke curls from
a lidless tenement window—
her parents burn the dirt
and slivers of glass
from their breakfast

Lea Nicole

You have been pushed into this world
without a dime, credit cards
cab fare to the station, or the names
and numbers of strange relatives and
relative strangers in Cleveland, Boston, Detroit—

you cry at the slap of birth
the cold air, hands and voices
caring without care
feeling without feeling.
Soon you will cry
in the gnaw for first milk
the trust of our eyes, the warmth of our hands
later to be left alone
and to be forgiven—

cry now, while someone listens
for all those beyond your dry tears
for those who know your name.

Happy Hour

Set'm up, Joe, let the serotonin flow
Kick in a little effexor gin fizz
A splash of paxil mash, a dash
Of bitters-block mix to nix my to-don't list
Yank my basal ganglia, nibble some frontal lobe
and slay this crazed mid-age braindrain plague

Zolofty are the heights, I know, trust me I know
Life is a one-shot-only prozac go-go-go
So, gimme the straight dopamine
Be a pal 'o my thalamus, my hip hippocampus
Since neither man norepinephrine can see
Behind my slurred, depakoted eyes all blurred—
Just one more for the one-way road I'm taking
'Cause, Joe, I'm shaken, really shakin', man,
not stirred

Shooting Pool with My Daughter
the Day After Her Release from Rehab

We take our rack
And find a table
Near the back of the place,
Just far away enough
From the others.
Four Albanians smoking,
Laughing, enjoying their game,
A white guy and a black guy,
Both about fifty,
Their own custom cues,
Oldschool buddies on a night out,
A young woman and two men,
Which one her boyfriend
It's not clear.
You wanna break, I ask.
No, go ahead.
My daughter is eighteen
But looks, what, twenty-five,
Her face hidden beneath
A layer of shame,
Thick eye shadow and
Her own cigarette smoke.
I chalk the stick I have pulled
From the customer rack.
I want a clean break.
Addressing the cueball,
I ramrod a ten-day stay
Of continuous guilt into
The racked diamond,
A sharp clack sending

Solids and stripes
Spinning in all directions.
Good job, dad, she says.
My mind leaves the green field
And Stevie Ray Vaughn
On the jukebox.
Where did it go wrong?
Down what pocket?
Off what padded rail?
When exactly, child, did we
Scratch on the eight?
Here, in this poolhall,
Beneath dimmed lights
Reflecting off perfect
Opposing balls and
A cloud of cigarette smoke,
We break into
The diamond of ourselves,
Spin out of control,
And find no bottom,
No pocket to hold us,
Only each other,
Each peering back,
Sizing up our next shot.

Malady of the Quotidian

The little prick quit trying weeks ago.
Each morning, the paper, your paper,
Flung like a garbagebag, dead by the curb
Or on the lawn, nowhere near the porch.
You hate him now, the shape of his head,
The way his bone-legs wiggle-waggle
The bike to pick up speed between houses.
That's it. You find yourself in the garage,
The sniveling boy kneeling before you
Executionstyle in front of the lawnmower
Beside paintcans half full of forgotten color.
"It's my paper, my paper, mine," you explain
Above his blubbering and pathetic apologies.
He'll promise you anything now, and it's
Suddenly hard to hate anything so weak.

You loose his collar, ease the hammer forward.
He bursts the side door open, a cool breeze
Finds you like a first gulp of bourbon.
You're empty, this place is strange,
The rafters above you swing a strong rope.
The hammer is notched back into place.
Whose hands are these? Where have you been?
What, just what, have you done?

Awakening

We learned our commandments
by breaking them,
scratching dry slate,
shoring rubbled fragments
after each hammer chink,
each chisel scrape,
simple work, blissful days,
hammered nights.
But then,
morning terror, doomed awake,
salt stinging in my beard,
the fortress now smoking at my feet—
black breeze sang
in the ruins like breath
on a stale reed,
the slate I lived beneath
      no more,

                   crumbled,
         dust.
I pulled from charred bone,
climbed black brick and beams,
hands blistering,
lungs heaving soot and ash,
eyes seared red.
Here, birthed forth amongst the dead,
I knew the hollow song
           of black wind—
razed in a city of fire,
burned, clean, unburned,
the world in which I listened,

nothing, not nothing,
now alive to live again.

The Composition Teacher Ponders Questions Posed by His Students at the Allen Correctional Institute

Most are routine.
Hey, a period go here?
demands Lamar,
a facts man
wanting rules, the straightline distance
through my class,
through me,
this whole motherfucking business.
William, though, the medicated one
whose neck and wrists
are ploughshared
by milkwhite mounds of scartissue,
hands me an essay
about his interest in astronomy
in which he tangentially mentions
how he accidently killed his infant daughter
during a narcotic blackout,
and asks in condemned, grainy pencil at the end,
This O.K., is'nt it?
I hold William's essay like I held
the one family dog the neighbor kids
stoned and booted for crapping on their lawn,
the dog I held in a bloody towel
we used to dry off the car,
the skin that formed his soft mouth
split to the eye socket,
his splintered ribs jutting the bloodmatted fur
like the jagged walls of a bombed city,
and I, knifed, muscleless, gutted dust,

I ask my mother in the vinyl frontseat
as we head to the vet's,
knowing but still asking,
He's gonna be alright, isn't he?

The Age of Song

Thumbs never find the thumbholes
      of your mittens,
and tying your own shoes is
as distant as next summmer's two-wheeler.
What about I'm big as you,
      you ask lately.
Oh, you will be, I answer,
hoping it's what you want me to say
and wondering what your hurry is.
At bedtime after story
      I sing to you,
my voice as odd and fragile
as a cricket's leg,
      This old man, he play one....
I cradle you, the tangled
hair of my arms gripping
on your cream skin,
and I sing, with no voice
to speak of, quietly,
this old singer a self-conscious one,
hidden from your mother
undressing in our room after work
and your sister coloring in hers.
Your doll-like fingers clutch
the frayed, papery blanket
my own mother made for me,
clowns and balloons and memory.
And you listen
to the only voice you hear,
this old man still rolling home,
until your lashes meet

and the world stops
to hear you breathe.
The words curl and close
in my throat, but I finish,
pulling the sound of myself
from places I know again
in voices I have heard before.

Elegy, for Josie

You were Sunday eggs
spattering in bacon grease,
bread fetched from Suchyta's
bakery lathered in real butter,
coffee lightened with
sweet heavy cream.
You were menthol cigarettes
as you folded clothes
during Oprah and Sixty Minutes,
simmering pot roast
surrounded by carrots
and redskin potatoes,
a chipped cup of coffee and an ashtray.
You were arms veined
with the weight of children
who had fallen asleep
on the living room floor
in front of Disney and Lassie,
Vicks Vapor Rub soothed
into a fevered chest,
cries of Come on, that's bullshit ref
at high school wrestling matches,
hands tethered with a gold ring
to a man who ran Johnny Walker Red,
prizefights, pool tables, and a pub of his own.
You rose from a life sunk deep
as the cobwebbed basement in Detroit
where you did the wash
for your three men.
You forgave nights left
bereft in the glare of TV and

crossword puzzles, comforted
by cats named for daughters
you never had, a blind dog
you fed chocolate,
and a rosary;
you forgave congealed plates
left on a deserted table
and asked forgiveness for sins
not even God was aware of.
At four foot eleven and 105 pounds,
you towered over our demons,
debt and doubt, addiction and death,
drawing one more draft for the customer
who helped sweep the barroom floor
or finding a blanket and a spot on the couch
in the apartment you made above your bar
for those too drunk, broke, or alone to go home.
You became chocolate eggs
in a grandchild's Easter basket,
a triumphant return from the toystore,
popsicles and Scooby-Do,
cakes of confirmation and communion,
one more quarter for pinball,
another favorite song on the jukebox,
one last rack of billiards in your pub's gameroom.
You were holder of children
and protector of stray cats
and mutts and mongrels who
stole from your cooler and cash box
but never took a thing you would mention.
When there was nothing good
to be found in a person
you found what was least bad.

You were gifts when it was not Christmas
and no one's birthday,
mother to sons and daughters
black and white, rich and poor,
the blessed and bottomed out,
buttons for a coat that
was given away long ago.
A year after you said your husband
would beat cancer,
you were the tearless greeting,
The big guy's gone.
You were the strength to pull me from
my father's disease-eaten body,
making me let go of his cool hand,
Let's go, we can't do anything more.
You were your last morning, December 22nd,
calling your brother in the next apartment over,
I'm not feeling well,
refusing the ambulance, the possibility
of inconveniencing paramedics,
alarming your cats,
I'm okay, I'm okay, I just don't feel well.
A few hours later your heart gave
after six decades, rivers of coffee and
two packs a day, serving happy hour
two-for-ones, a husband married
to a Ping five wood and nine ball,
ringing out the registers at 2 a.m. after last call,
pork chops and pie and ice cream
and half a night's sleep.
Two days after I kissed your cool forehead
at the ICU, signed papers willing your eyes
and skin and bone to any stranger in need,

we open your presents without you,
underwear and clothes for my wife and me,
games for your grandkids, the kind
you would be playing with them now,
careful to never win,
and a rawhide bone
for the family dog, no one left out
                              but you.
Today we bury you next
to your bartender husband.
Today we lift you, smaller than
your eleven year old granddaughter,
and we carry a weight heavier
than kegs of Stroh's, cases of mozzarella,
corned beefs or mortgage payments.
Today is black coffee with no cream,
crusts of unbuttered bread,
pork chops with no fat,
tea without honey or whiskey,
a foamy draft left on the bar
without your signature "all-righty-didy then."
Today, we hear your last last-call,
and we, your family of customers,
do not want to leave but must go home,
nothing more we can do,
closing time, the last penny counted,
our glasses empty, a few tips left on the bar,
coolers stocked for tomorrow,
floors swept and mopped,
lights dimmed, front and back doors locked,
thank you, we'll see you, Josie, good-bye.

The East Enders

We were dumb about our stupidity,
broadcasting it, lime suspenders
Jacking up plaid polyester, calling
Card hucklebuck huckster dumbness.
We passed off flatulance for wit,
Bazooka Joe for wisdom,
Mastercard and VISA for security,
Lawn gnome for art,
Peroxide and mascara for beauty,
Crosswords for intellect,
Collection baskets for religion,
Light beer for discipline,
Mag wheels for status,
Stitches for respect,
Perfume for love,
T-bones for the good life.
We worked diligently at nothing
Anyone would remember or
Pay a decent wage for,
Proudly produced perishable goods,
Eagerly consumed generic or what
Could only be bought in bulk,
And openly mocked those fatassed
Bigwigs who docked our pay and
Planned our daily obsolescence.
We wondered in earnest what dogs
Would say if they could talk,
Where doughnut holes went,
Who made God and the first catcher's glove,
If the Incredible Hulk could whip Godzilla,
When exactly leisure suits went out of style,

Whether tomatoes were fruit or vegetable,
Why there was no number eleventy-leven.
Reflection for us was a split second
Revelation next to a nightclub urinal.
If we harmed anyone, it was ourselves
And we never felt a goddamned thing.

Lionfish

Aquarium beautiful
stupidly maleficent
gaping lips
blind to its own barbs,
daggerheaded begger
and eyeless king—
as a boy on a Miami fishing pier
I saw one hurled headlong
overboard with the cleanings.
Angelwing and needlecrown
useless as it dropped to the water,
abdicating into
a shadowy froth of parasites
darting for an easy meal—
poison chum, quilled cancer,
usurping shadows
kissing their last meal—

Shouldered on crumbling pavement
I look for a man with my face,
mouth pulled taut against the undertow,
bones worn like reef,
teeth catching at shadows
flown to the depths of my sea

About the Poet

John Jeffire was born in Detroit. His debut novel, *Motown Burning*, won Grand Prize in the 2005 Mount Arrowsmith Novel Competition and the 2007 Independent Publishing Awards Gold Medal for Regional Fiction. His stories, poems, and essays have appeared in *Parenting*, *The English Journal* and *America*.

Last summer, an excerpt from his second novel, *River Rouge*, won first prize in the 2007 Springfed Arts Metro Detroit Fiction Contest. For more on the author and his work, visit his website at www.johnjeffire.com.

About the *Living Detroit* Series

Pledged to preserve the history of the city of Detroit and the memories of its residents, Aquarius Press presents the *Living Detroit* Book Series. Look for this special collection at your local bookstores and Amazon.com.

- -

Mail Order Form

	Qty.	Total
Stone+Fist+Brick+Bone by John Jeffire $14.99	___	____
Eyes on Fire: Witnesses to the Detroit Riot $24.99 of 1967	___	____

Subtotal $_____

Shipping ($2.50 + $1 for each additional book) $_____

Amount Enclosed $_____

Name_____

Shipping Address_____

_____

Phone_____

Email_____

Make checks payable to Aquarius Press, PO Box 23096, Detroit, MI 48223
($30 fee on returned checks; no returns on books after 30 days from purchase.)